A gift given,
A gift taken
collection
of poems
~ Plus

A gift given,
A gift taken

collection

of poems

~ Plus

JULIET BARRIFFE

Contents

Acknowledgment 1
Dedication 3

"When God Is In The Mix" ______________________

His Mystical Touch 6
The Desired Vessel 7
Songs In My Heart..9
He Intercedes 10
How Forgetful...11
The Praying Power 12
Beyond His Blessings..14
The Richness Of His Love....................................15
I Am Thankful, Lord..16
The Song, The Voice, The Words.....................17
The Incomparable One 18
Hope For Glory Land 20
A Seed Sown, A Seed Grown 21
His Child, Christ's Child..22
The Gardener...23
Sisters In Christ...24
The Christian Soldiers...25
The Unwelcome Guest..27
The Whispering Voice Of Angels 28
"In The Morning" 30

I'm Saying 32
Our Ocean Chandelier..................................33
Expression Of Love 34
My Escape...35
Came By The Wind 36
Stop The Love Song 37
Demonstrate Your Love...............................38
My Starlight 39
Let's Dance...40
Loving Love 41
My Deliverer 42
To Be Loved By You 43
A Love Like No Other.................................44
Memories Of Butterflies..............................46
It's God's Doing 47
Define Life 49
My Pearls 51
Unshackled 52
The Garden Of Roses..................................53
Everything Has Its Place..............................54
His Work Of Art...55
When Beautiful Is Beautiful 56
Life Is A Journey 57
The Troubled Soul......................................58
No Mercy By Thy Self.................................59
The Strength Of Friendship 61
Besetting Pride 62
The First Hello, To Forever 63
The Caribbean Sun 64

Dedicated To Mothers

It's Mom And Her Heart Of Gold 66
From A Daughter's Heart 67
We Appreciate You, Mom 68
Her Children Called Her Blessed 69
Motherhood 70
Mothers 71
Dear Mother 72
I Behold You, Mother 73
Pray On, Mothers 74

Dedicated To Fathers

The Strength Of A Father 76
A Father's Prayer 77
"Our Heavenly Father" 78

"It's Us Lord"

We Are The Product 80
Striving To Do Right 81
We Heard The Drums! 82

When This Earth Is No Longer Home

Cry Not For Me 85
God Is There 86
Don't Take It To Heart 87
Farewell To A Dad 88
A Missed Loved One 89

Bonus ~ Stories

The Thoughts Of A Tree 91
To Be Deceived Or Not To Be Deceived 94

About The Author...108

ACKNOWLEDGMENT

"In everything give thanks, for this is the will of God in Christ Jesus" 1 Thessalonians 5:18.

It is with this grateful heart of mine that I give all honor and praise to the one who kept me, and bestowed upon me a gift that I thought I was not capable of moving forth with; He is my Lord and Savior.

To my daughters, Nieoka and Nakedi Gayle, who are my motivation to press on each day. Nieoka, I thank you for always answering my calls for good reasons. Nakedi, my coach who keeps reminding me with "You can do it, Mommy." My granddaughter and my cheerleader, Naelani Brown, who has high hopes for my writing -- she, at a young age, began to applaud her Nana, by giving a shout out for her favorite poems. My grandson, Jessih, to whom I am Nana Darling. My mother, Hazel Lambert, who has been there when I needed her most, I thank you. My sister, Elaine Harriott, and brothers, Derrick and Donavan, who kept the siblings' love alive. The family members, who have been applauding and praying for me, you know who you are. I appreciate and love you.

To the anointed man of God, my pastor, Dr. Rev. Cecil B Stone, I thank you for your many prayers and encouragement all these years. Even when I refused to stepped forward, you believed in me and the gifts that the Father has deposited within me. You, continued to keep on praying for my light to shine.

I will be amiss not applauding my three sisters in Christ who have gone up and beyond to publicize poems I wrote. To Maxine Frazer, I thank you for putting my poem on t-shirts and for printing copies at your own expense in my early years of writing.

Herberta Bosley, who has been showcasing my work and who also kept me thinking by giving to me topics to construct into poems, I thank you for believing in me, and, also for keeping your prayers for me afloat.

The Rev. Wendy Modeste, thank you for your friendship and your professional touch in reference, to my writing, and the encouragements and counsel you have given.

To professor Bill Mazza, of LaGuardia college, I thank you for your encouragement to pursue writing.

My Springfield Gardens United Methodist Church family, you are many, however, you know who you are. I thank you for your gifts of note books, diaries, and books from other authors, but most of all I cherish your prayers and love. God's continuous blessings to all.

To my readers, I thank you for choosing this book for your reading. I pray, as you venture through the pages, that one or more poems will attract your interest and speak to your heart; and will you then please consider it as my gift to you.

DEDICATION

I dedicate this book in recognition to the many gifts in the body of Christ as it is stated in Romans 12:6-8. "We have different gifts, according to the grace given to each of us. If your gift is prophesying, then prophesy in accordance with your faith; if it serving, then serve; if it is teaching, then teach; if it is to encourage, then give encouragement; if it is giving, then give generously; if it is to lead, do it diligently; if it is to show mercy, do it cheerfully."

Are you uncertain about what your gift might be? Pray about it; ask the Lord to make it plain. Listen to your heart and that still, soft voice in your ears; are you listening? Your answer is there.

"WHEN GOD IS IN THE MIX"

Rejoice always, pray continually, give thanks in
all circumstance…
Thes. 5:16-18

HIS MYSTICAL TOUCH

I felt His hands upon me as I stood among worshipers, worshiping Him. I felt His touch, that mystical touch of one whom many say is not real.

With His touch I felt comforted, my Savior's touch felt reassuring; To complain of a touch that is unlike any other would be stifling. With His touch came confidence, security, and joy.

Along came the release of a body weight that once felt like tons of rocks accumulated together; as each rock rolled away, I found strength increased in many ways. The strength of lifting my hands to worship and pray, strength to stomp my feet and crush the devil in the clay.

With a touch, that special touch that came from our heavenly King. I say, friends, should you feel his hands on your shoulders, don't brush Him off but pray that it enfolds you. Your healing is possible with His hands upon you. His gentle mystical touch is not seen but felt. Do you feel that sensation going through your being? Embrace it!

THE DESIRED VESSEL

Lord! When you placed your hands upon me, I knew that I would never be the same in that moment I become your servant; since that day I only have one aim, to serve you, Lord

An empty vessel longing to be filled by you

My soul's desire is to serve you, Lord

To do your perfect will, to work each day in honoring your name

This is my sole desire

Lord! I do not seek to claim glory

My only desire is to be under your control; I know that you alone are worthy; and I seek a place for this longing in my soul

My soul's desire is to be used

An empty vessel longing to be filled by you

My soul's desire is to serve you, Lord

To do your perfect will, to work each day in honoring your name

This is my sole desire

My soul's desire is to be used
An empty vessel longing to be filled by you
My soul's desire is to serve you, Lord
To do your perfect will, to work each day
in honoring your name
This is my sole desire

My soul's desire is to be used
An empty vessel longing to be filled by you
My soul's desire is to serve you, Lord
To do your perfect will, to work each day
in honoring your name
This is my sole desire, Jesus
This is my sole desire

SONGS IN MY HEART

There are days I feel so strong, my heart overflows with many songs.

Songs of praise, of prayer, and even songs of forgiveness of things I might have done. You know! A lie, a little cuss, and maybe anger as well as lust. Whatever the reason, my Father holds no grudge. He has known what I would be like before I was born. Therefore, He had a plan that would enhance my life. He sent a lamb that was pure and clean to the slaughter for you and me. Knowing that I am, able to partake of this lamb, it's a blessing being provided for. I am happy I will not be thirsty or hungry anymore. His package of grace, mercy, and peace are inclusive within His love; Praises be to the Lord.

There are days I feel so strong, my heart overflows with many songs.

HE INTERCEDES

He intercedes for me; that is what the Spirit does.

Oh! What burden to overcome. It brings a feeling of joy and receptive desires when I think of what my Lord and Savior will do if I only take my burden to Him. No feeling have I felt can fulfill my desires of wants and needs of any earthly request.

What a plan, what a master plan my Lord has for me if only I let Him intercede. I will take my burden to Him. I will let Him be everything for me. I will let Him do what I can't do for myself, that's why I am happy, He intercedes for me. Praise the Lord! Praises for my God. Praising you, Savior, for your master plan.

HOW FORGETFUL

How forgetful we are, not remembering to pause each morning for just a second to say good morning to our Lord and Savior before our busy day begins

How forgetful we are that we are at the altar on the day of worship;
We talked to Him, we praised Him for His goodness.
We asked for …
We told Him about … Yet! Today we forget to pray

How forgetful we are that the future is not promised to us, to no, no, no one. However, our Lord extends His grace to see you through, to see me through.

How forgetful we are that
Our Father, Our Lord, Our Savior
Is always the same. He will never forget us. He will forgive us if we asked.

How forgetful we are that the Savior loves us always, no matter what. But we should remember to commune with Him perpetually.

THE PRAYING POWER

Why do I pray?

The word is, "the prayer of the righteous availed much"

Am I righteous? I guess not,

Not when one's baggage is smudged and heavy, ha! the Savior cares not

The compassionate and gracious Lord, turned not a deaf ear to the unrighteous one's cry. He said, "Come as you are my child, there is room at the cross

Don't look for condemnation from me, there is none.

Tell me of your troubles and your fears, I will not reveal it to the world; what I'll do is give you, peace.

A peace that will comfort you,

pray and believe in your heart"

Why do we pray, how do we pray?
Why do we pray, what do we say?

How do we pray? Pray kneeling, sitting, standing or lying down -- it does not matter. He wants us to be real and true;

We can whisper it, scream it, moan it, or just be silent in His presence. He will understand, shoo! Don't you know He is God? Pray for your joy, pray away your sorrows, pray away your pain; pray for your sisters, and your brothers, pray for the parents and yes, the children too; and those who are dissolute, speak on their behalf. A prayer for your enemies is acceptable too. Prayers binding the strong-man probing this earth will not go unanswered

Speak to Jesus, tell Him, ask Him, He will take care of your request.

Why do I pray?

I pray for God is my light from darkness,

My joy from sorrow, my richness from poverty, He is my rock in the valley, He is my today away from yesterday.

He is my song, my dance, my music, my all and all.

Why do I pray?

I pray for I know the King who owns everything, He is the comforter of us who diligently worship Him.

He is God the Father, Son, and Holy Spirit. My reason for praying.

BEYOND HIS BLESSINGS

Beyond the blessings of the Most-High, there are none better to behold than His love. With His love

He gives comfort to those who diligently seeks Him. He heals those whose faith withstand their unbelief. He will be there when all others leave you standing.

When you focus on the blessings of the Most-High and His abundant love, there is nothing unreachable.

Beyond the blessings of the Most-High

there are none better to behold.

He keeps the sun shining. He gives light where there is darkness. He gives mercy when others are mercy-less. He gives love when you feel love-less. He gives grace unmeasurable, how abundant is His blessings.

Beyond the blessing of the Most-High, there are none better to behold.

He gives the flow of quenchable water so that we will thirst no more. He nurtures the tree of our life with the fulfillment of His promises and His love.

Beyond the blessings of the Most-high, there are none better to behold.

THE RICHNESS OF HIS LOVE

The price of sorrow I will pay, carrying the guilt of not doing the will of my Lord.He asked me not for the impossible for His desire is not to burden the ones He loves. He said He loves me in so many ways. He gives me the freedom of knowing how to pray. He comforts my heart with melody of songs; He poeticizes my heart with words of scriptures; He enfolds me with His love. He tells me it's everlasting as, long as I take Him at His word. His love is always there and I find peace in its unconditional way. There are times I forget to tell Him I love and thank Him for the faith He has given me and my aim is to serve Him. Oh! What a love to have -- a love that will comfort me all my days. He cares not if we are young or old, attractive or not, rich or poor; As a matter of fact, He is rich abundantly. He told me He will always take care of me. Yea! What price of sorrow I will pay if I don't exercise my Jesus' will today.

I AM THANKFUL, LORD

I thank you, Lord, for all that you have been giving me -- the love I have possessed to conquer all that came against me, the strength to worship and adore you, the power to put the devil behind me.

I thank you, Lord, that I can live ever thereafter for the promise of eternal life you have given when you died to set us free.

I thank you, Lord. How can I not thank you for the pain you endured making sure that we will be free?

I thank you Lord now that you are living within me. There is much to throw away and much to repair now that you are in my life. You have done so much; I make my choice to follow you.

I thank you, Lord that I came to the knowledge of thee. Now that you are my everything, I just want to thank you, Lord.

THE SONG, THE VOICE, THE WORDS

The echoing words of the song, *"I'm Gonna Be Ready."* Have awakened my emotions, hearing the soothing sound of the singer's voice uttering my prayer in her song. It brought to light my thoughts of preparation for journeying through life. That passible every day trial or trouble or perhaps that unexpected calling to that spiritual journey…

The journey on a mission to serve without reservations

The journey of interceding, praying in faith on others behalf

The journey of forgiveness and love when the situation required the opposite

The journey of strength and perseverance although weakness is conflicting your being

Yes! The words of the song reflect a turnaround in life, from a path of troubles and discouragement to that of a meaningful one

The self-reflection of the song is -- I pray, Lord, prepare me for whatever may come my way. You see, I, too, *"I'm Gonna be Ready."*

THE INCOMPARABLE ONE

There is one who sits on His clouds of throne, raises His mantle each night, and uncovers the stars that shine with countless sparks. He places the moon as the globe that manages the earth surface at every angle, being a light in darkened nights, it is, able to showcase its many features according to the Master's calendar within the atmosphere. And so, it is within the nights, the gift of God, high in the above, yet mindful of us here on the earth's surface. Yeah! A grateful heart is not of the massive, there in the dark when He shines His light. In the dark, many deeds are not of the fruitfulness but of bittersweet and sometimes of sour grapes. You know the wine is not always sweet!

Say! That's why He is the incomparable one who didn't hide the availability of the sun to flourish our every need to survive, by nurturing the earth's surface at a balance according to His calendar that's not known to us. Consider the sunlight that helps nurture our body and is damaging, too; Yes! It can be bittersweet or tarnished. Ah! The prunes do lose their texture.

Now, let's consider the incomparable one who is magnificent and awesome in all His ways. His capabilities are unimaginable and His gifts are rich and flourishing in the acceptable hearts of man, us, His people. Yet! Be it bittersweet and sad, for death is the departure from life. Yes! He is forever; be the incomparable one.

I am heading for glory land with my Lord.

Though the enemy is trying his best that I fail the test of being right with my Lord. I will not yield to take a rest that might cast me a permanent rest, and give the enemy the chance to prevail within my thoughts. I am pushing on, no matter what! I have a report of accomplishment within my Savior grace to tell. I have a testimony; He has taken me on a journey. I wouldn't be on if it had not been the great Divine.

The enemy had loved me; I know he had. He had me in the palm of his hands. However, a greater love than his binds my heart. He tried hooking my heels many times but I haven't fallen, being caught by the great Divine. Now, I am standing tall and holding on to the hands that pulled me through with grace.

A SEED SOWN, A SEED GROWN

Can't you see what the enemy has done?

He has given kids the right over their moms and dads.

He has tied the hands of the mothers and fathers who will not let their children go out on a limb.

Don't abuse to be accused, let love be the banner and correct in a timely manner

Make your pledge to be your best with example and in honor

A seed sown is a seed grown, it's a direction that a child will not depart from.

But in case peer pressure gets in the way, let example and encouragement prevail.

Children are sensitive people and so were the disciples who were led by the great teacher

He sowed His seed in the personality of the twelve and watered it in the manner it was perceived; they became doers and livers of the word because faith and example is the Master's way.

Mothers and fathers, take a hint; be leaders in your children's life.

The map of life is the Bible; they will never get lost when they discover that Jesus is the way.

HIS CHILD, CHRIST'S CHILD

I am God's child
I am precious in His sight
Don't tell me I am not bright, when I
> know I am glowing with His light
I am glowing with God's light
I have a hanker to know Him more
I was told He has been loving me, and
> keeping me evermore
The reason why I know I am always
> within His light
I am precious in His sight

THE GARDENER

There is a garden deep within our soul no one can see, but the enhancing of a fragrance that can be had by those we encounter

The fragrance of love, understanding, and compassion are there to enhance others, because the Gardener of our lives has attended to our garden deep within

The sweetness of our garden has over flown in the sanctuary each time we shout praises that glorify the name of the Most High.

The freshness of the believer's faith is visible to the eyes. The spirit embedded within us absorbs the blessings we shout to the Father, the Gardener of our lives. Each member is blessed and the blessing flows to those we encounter within our walk each day.

They will know that we have worshipped our Lord with all our being because the Holy Spirit will not frail away within the day but will flourish within us for more days than we can say.

The believers are not the only ones to be blessed. An unbelieving soul, or possible a lonesome heart be touched, unsmiling face be brightened when they witness the compassion and the everlasting nurturing from the Gardener of our soul in our lives. The families of the sanctuary of love testifying of His greatness.

That's how Jesus', the Gardener of our lives, love overflows.

SISTERS IN CHRIST

How do you say thank you to someone who does more than words can say?

How do you say, "I appreciate you" when appreciation is less than the spoken words the heart wants to display?

Therefore, I sum it up this way: loving you sisters brings forth the Jesus in me. Being sisters in Christ, we stand together. With sisters such as you, who are encouraging, loving, prayerful, and nurtures the friendship of sister-hood, others will get the notion that Jesus is our Father and His way is love.

THE CHRISTIAN SOLDIERS

Dressed up and ready

To go on the battle-field of the warrior's ground.

Not a tear had been shed,

Each soldier believed in victory over defeat.

Each soldier walking behind the other, stepping in his or her shadow.

How comforting, knowing there is strength being together.

"What is your branch of service?"

 One soldier asked of the other.

"I am on the mission team,"

one proud and brave answered.

"We are aiming to gather the lost sheep back to the shepherd," added the sergeant.

The prayer warriors shouted from behind,

"We have your backs, we are praying for you."

And from others,

"We are the reserves. We believe in the Holy fight and its reasons. We will fill in when needed; we are on the side line."

Dressed up and ready to go on the battle-field of the warrior's ground.

With everything intact, all prepared for an attack from the enemies.

Salvation in place,

Righteousness is perfected,

Truth is ready to be delivered,

The sword, sharpened to perfection.

We believe in victory over defeat,

We stand strong for our Chief has our backs.

We called Jesus!

    Jesus!

      Jesus!

        Jesus!

THE UNWELCOME GUEST

I stopped by, sister, to attend to your needs; I will try my best to make you neat and clean. Yes, your sickness -- it's hard to cope with; the pain that is physical and the situations that are mental are driving you to the extreme. I would like to make you comfortable in every way. I brought someone along with me, too -- the great Physician, Jesus. I like you to meet Him, also. We stopped by sister, Jesus and I, to attend to your needs. You rejected the offer of attending to your needs and the healing you would have received. Jesus is not mad at you. He loves you just the same. He wants you to come to Him for your healing any time of day.

He felt the touch of angels, but he did not respond; he thought it was his dead folks from beyond. The voices of angels whispered in his ears while he drowned in the depth of sleep

"The sun is very hot."

Yet he responded not to the voice of angels

Angels on their assigned mission, being persistent to do their Master's bid,

shook the unbelieving husband of a saved wife. Unsaved he is but covered by the grace of the Heavenly King, through a daughter who choose to believe and follow Her Lord and King.

With voices and touch from angels that became forceful and strong, the unsaved one could not help but respond to the words,

"the sun is very hot."

He woke to find not the radiant sun of the sky, but a smoking room that would have been his tomb. His lunch became tared on the stove and waited to explode, but the angels of the Lord shined the light of survival in his mind and he responded just in time;

Yet! The unsaved husband gave credit to his dead folks beyond.

"Lord, have mercy on this unbeliever," cried the saved wife, "he does not understand that he is covered by you, The Christ."

"IN THE MORNING"

As the morning light showed itself through the windows, my sleepy eyes began to open to the sunlight that shone so brightly on this early spring morning. I became alert and embraced the morning and the joy it brought to my heart that I was alive one more day to embark upon what lies ahead.

I slowly slid off my bed and then fell on my knees to honor the one who made this day, this morning possible. As I prayed, I heard the birds chirp their morning song so sweetly. I took a breath, then exhaled. "Within this day, this morning, and for the other mornings I will see, I give thanks always to thee, our Father."

Continue your love to those who know you,
your righteousness to the upright in heart.
Psalm 36:10

I'M SAYING

If the sun should say to the earth
We are not compatible
What soil of fruitless bearing there will be
If the moon should say to the night
I am graceful without you
Then where would the beauty of the moon lie
If the flesh should say to the blood
Away with you
Then where would the body be
If I were you and you were me
Would you erase the possibility of a prosperous life
Because I could be the reverse of you and you of me

Isn't love a beautiful thing
In spite of color or race
Love has no boundaries or
Negative feelings to erase
See me with your heart ~ I'm saying to you
The heart will behold the foundation of my soul
That your eyes cannot see
Then love will be what love should be
Not black or white, but you and me
As we are created to be

OUR OCEAN CHANDELIER

Two eyes locked and became one

Time stood still as distant drums beat to the rhythmic pounding of the hearts that only the two can hear

Time moved on as the distance between the two drew closer

While hands touched, their hearts beat to a dance taking place within; only the two hearts in motion were aware of

Starlight became their candle-lights, the ocean surface gave a reflection of a crystal chandelier as the moonlight shone and placed their hearts in motion for love

Love of what they had and will to share

If it were only permissible that time would last forever.

EXPRESSION OF LOVE

Express yourself, my dear, let your words speak volumes to my heart.

Let your emotion reveal your love, with your love there is no reason to be sad; come closer, my love, and let me enfold you into my being. Trust your heart, knowing that the Savior has allowed us two to become as one. Yes, my dear, express yourself, continue to let your words speak volumes to my heart.

MY ESCAPE

Love is an escape from being lonely
Affection is an escape from being
self-centered
Finding is an escape from seeking
Touching is an escape from being untouchable
Seeking is an escape from the unknown
Finding, loving, knowing, and touching you grows
into affection and turns into love
Know my escape is you!

CAME BY THE WIND

The wind has blown in many directions and it has blown you to me.

Since the day you came into my life, it has never been the same for me.

You have comforted me with your love and kindness as God ordained it to be; you have lifted me to the height that I would like me to be.

It seems that God has made no mistake sending you to me; I would like us to be forever, you know, until eternity.

However, tell me we can get down on our knees and give thanks to the One who sent you to me.

STOP THE LOVE SONG

How do you listen to a love song after the love is gone?

The memories of the moments once shared. The jokes and the laughter, the kisses and the hugs that followed.

The time we became one in body and soul, the time we separated because of misunderstandings; reunion was possible, we were each other's fool.

How do you listen to a love song after the love is gone? Seized away by death.

It is said that love lives on after the person is gone. But! How can you touch, feel and embrace someone who is not in your arms?

Tell me! How do you listen to a love song when the reason is gone?

DEMONSTRATE YOUR LOVE

Demonstrate to me the meaning of your love; show me your love by taking my hand and leading me. Make me believe you are strong. Embrace me when emotions speak to you with an uncertain tone; nurture me with words of confidence and strength. Let me not drown in doubts of the future, but let us flow in the river of prosperity. Show me the meaning of your love so that I may confess that God has sent you to me.

MY STARLIGHT

I have searched for you these many years, until time has taken its toll.

I have never thought I would find the starlight I have searched for in the eyes of someone so astounding.

Your eyes of light make your face so bright; I want to glow along with you.

So! For the years that have passed and gone, I say farewell to them and welcome to you. Today is now and you are here with me. Therefore, tomorrow can welcome us as one as I extend my heart to you. And I thank God for letting this dream come through.

LET'S DANCE

I want us to dance our love song

together

For the rest of our days

When our feet cease to move to the sound of the beat, let's make our hearts take over in one accord while our eyes lock together in their every move, as our hands touch to reveal the rhythm in our hearts

If I should be the one who remain in this world after our lives have taken its toll

I will forever dance to our love song in my heart.

LOVING LOVE

Love should not be jealousy

Love should not be of strife

Love is not taking others' property

Love is you, love is me living in unity

Loving is loving without causing pain

Love should not be affliction

Love should not be wrath

Love is knowing that love is a profit that can be deposited and love interest is there to gain

Love is obeying God's commandment of loving each other

Love is God within us

Love is God, God is love. Love!

MY DELIVERER

I have found my deliverer

I have found my friend

I have found that someone who will love me to the end

He buys me not roses

He buys me not pearls

But what he gives to me is confidence and love to face the world

My days are special because I have someone who loves me unconditionally.

I am not selfish, I will introduce him to you.

His name is Jesus.

TO BE LOVED BY YOU

It's a blessing, it's a praise to be loved by you, try as I did to love you the way you love me, I will never measure up; Your love is perfect from beginning to no end; whereas, my King, my love gets smudged with doubts and fears even though I know the extent of your love, my King. I had doubts of the forgiveness of my sins my Lord, which you have willingly forgiven when you gave your life for me. Oh! It's a blessing, it's a praise to be loved by you.

A LOVE LIKE NO OTHER

To say I love you has become a love song on my lips and music to my heart

To wake up and embrace you each day have become my pleasure

To walk along with you on my mind each moment of a given day has made me realize that life is embracing and your love is rewarding

This joy of loving you! It has placed in my life an everlasting desire of being your child with a willing heart to do your will and extending your love to others; I have yearned for a love so refreshing and real, a love no man can steal, I found such love came from only you, my heavenly King. I will continue to sing your praise, I will continue to honor your love; I will honor your name for you are worthy to be adored. To say I love you has become a song -- a song on my lips and music to my heart.

To wake up and embrace you each day have become my pleasure

To walk along with you on my mind each moment of a given day let me realize life is embracing and your love is a wonderful thing and rewarding

Your love is a wonderful thing, my King

Your love is a wonderful thing, my Savior

Your love is wonderful and you make each moment possible in loving you, my King. I love you, my Savior!

MEMORIES OF BUTTERFLIES

The smell of freshness lingered in the air as the early days of spring began to bring forth new life to the surface; as the cold days of winter began to take its rest. The flowers began to decorate the earth's surface; whereas the trees put forth its new leaves and buds; it's the season of new birth. The feeling of life anew bubbled within my being as I embraced the morning and the actions of the birds that came into view while I sat on a nearby bench. I saw the birds perched on their chosen branch of their selected tree while chirping sweet sound to the ears. I viewed a lone butterfly which danced to the sound of the birds on that beautiful early spring morning. The sight of the butterfly brought memories of an encounter I once had, which had taken my breath away, on a beautiful spring day on a Caribbean Island. The view then was breathtaking; it had appeared as though the heavens had opened-up and poured out countless butterflies in the path. The butterflies danced around in their glory of yellow as if they knew they had the same designer. They moved around in motions, displaying their freedom of being there for the moment on that beautiful spring morning on the Caribbean Island of Jamaica, where the butterflies danced around for me.

IT'S GOD'S DOING

As I sat in the distance under the covering of a man-made structure of a building,

I was fortunate to have the view of the ocean that was not very far away.

The view of ships gliding by captivated my interest, as well as that of the seagulls diving for their big catch of the day. The desire of dipping my hands in the cold and inviting water was great to my imagination, and so was the possibility of sieving the sand through my fingers but distance has kept me away. However, my eyes had seen it all and my mind gravitated to the wonders of our almighty King. Then I thought of yesterday.

Yesterday, I viewed the ocean like a rebellious and cantankerous person.

I saw the tides wail like a fierce warrior fighting to the end. While the sand became prey to the gushing wind that blew it to and fro, there was no room for friendliness; even the seagulls stayed away.

Today, the ocean appeared calm and satisfied, like a baby resting in its mother's arm, under the strength of the sunlight that gave the effect of diamonds afloat on the ocean surface. While above the upper atmosphere, the covering of blue and white clouds promised a calm and settled day.

My heart pounded with appreciation for the greatness of the One whom I serve. What will I do, what will we do without the One who is so profound? The creator of the height and depth and the in between. He is above it all. How great is He who is our God, our King who has created all things?

DEFINE LIFE

What is life! What is life?

Is it breathing, touching, feeling, seeing, or smelling?

Is it coming and going to and from?

Or is it knowing you exist, you know, just being?

What is life? What is life? Really, what is life?

I want to know!

I take it, it is the above and more.

Is it the effect of our organs; the flowing of the blood?

Eating right and living right, ha!

But are we doing that?

Does it not contribute to life?

What is life, What! What is life?

Is it having riches immensely?

Is it taking from the rich and giving to the poor?

Or is it about loving, giving, and caring about yourself, but others more?

Is it helping the weak when you are strong? Or is it kicking them down and trampling them to the ground?

What is life? What is life? Tell me, I really want to know.

Is it being your brother's or sister's keeper?

Is it helping a child by building him or her up, or is it taking away whatever substance of innocence God gave His children?

What is life! What is life?

Is it living right and serving Christ until you die?

Is that your life?

MY PEARLS

When did the days and years pass me by? I was not in a trance; I watched them grow up. I know. Ha! Years ago, my mind revealed to me; it was years ago they were running around carefree and playful, being happy to be mommy's girls. I had the honor of control and it felt so good. They were my girls to groom, encourage, and pamper. I could say then, baby-girls come here, is your homework finished, baby-girls stay there, eat your meal. Yes, mommy! Their response was that of music to my ears.

Today, I glance at the ladies I birthed and groomed; it reflected a sense of pride and accomplishment of their receiving the reward of self-perseverance in their lives. The richness of their identity as a woman let me realize I did not strive in vain. The promises of the Savior have flourished within the lives of a mother and her daughters, her pearls -- the ladies, the mothers of the generation in process.

UNSHACKLED

I stand strong with what I was given. However, it's not my strength;

I am a woman designed to be victorious in many ways;

However, my outer pasture is not my crowning glory but that of my inner being. I was held hostage by the deception of the world in my mind, restrained and kept captive within my thoughts until the shackles of my mind became loose by the inner power and strength I gained from the table of deliverance that was set before me while I was laying on my bed of thorns.

I concurred within my thoughts -- those of victory and of freedom, free of my adversaries and the shackles that kept me bound. As I stand within the clouds of prosperity, crowned with the crown of victory, freed from the shackles of hindrance and doubts, I am liberated from the burden of weakness. I am now delivered into my achievements. I am free! I am wearing my crown of victory; I am being redeemed.

My outer pasture is not my crowning glory, but that of my inner being which absorbed the glory of the King. I am free from my bondage and from the shackles of this world.

THE GARDEN OF ROSES

As fresh bloom roses are we, sisters from our Father up above.

We have grown, bloomed in His words of wisdom, understanding and His love. As sisters we stand in unity. As sisters with faith, we have absorbed the flow of the spirit. As sisters we gravitate to His love and the love of each other. The roses are delicate flowers in their array of colors and grades. So were we at one time or the other, our weakness and fears at various levels. Now we are like a watered garden of roses blooming together, Sisters standing together to be the best we can be for each other,

Sisters flowing over with love embracing others.

Should drought come upon the garden of roses, we will not wither and crumble because of the drought that befall us. The garden of roses, the bond of sister-ship will hold fast to the One who brought us together.

EVERYTHING HAS ITS PLACE

The creatures of this earth have their stories to tell; only if we, the humans, stand still and remember not to yell.

The birds have their song to whistle or tweets to help us be in awe of God's miraculous creation and His plan to enhance our appreciation of Him being the creator.

It's so wonderful how everything has its place -- the hills, the valley, the grass, and even the barren land, not to mention the rivers and the sea, oh! even the creatures of various types and breeds. The human, us men and women, we hold a special place in His heart.

If you should ever feel lost or disconnected, remember God gave everything its place including you. Your place in Him you will never lose should you wander away from Him. The arms of the Savior are always open wide to welcome you to the place where you belong.

As for the creatures that have their story to tell, it may not make sense to you; their movements and cry are foreign to those who do not give them much thought or spell; voice your stories, human that is in the race, tell of His wonderous arms that enfold you when you gave up hope and wandered. Though you were lost and out of place, the Father extended His open arms, His grace. Tell the story, tell your story of how you found your place.

HIS WORK OF ART

As I walked along the trail in the park, the time of year when the color of green amongst the trees of which the leaves makes their transition from being green to the color granted them, the path ended there on the trail where I was presented with an awesome moment of nature.

I have stepped in a display of nature of which the Creator, the ultimate artist, was showcasing His magnificent work.

I became captivated by the scenery that hypnotized my eyes with its beauty. I saw the clouds with their array of colors reflected among the trees which embraced and kissed the acceptance of their beauty.

I witnessed the color scheme of the artist's spiritual handiworks within the clouds and its reflections upon the pond which has its added incentive of the likes of the swan gliding around while the butterfly flew around, unaware of the setting it's in and the picturesque view that was left in my mind.

The embrace of emotion and the overflow of gratitude for the artwork of the Master's hands -- the memory became the canvas of my heart where such beauty is stored and the sentiment is hard to erase.

How beautiful is beauty when beautiful stays beautiful;

How beautiful is beauty when beautiful shows its beauty in the heart of man;

How beautiful is beauty when beauty covers the faces of man, and beauty is there to see, as it is within the land; when beauty is all the heart of man will see; when beauty is the very core of the land, and can be so of man.

LIFE IS A JOURNEY

Life is a journey that tosses us to and fro

Sometimes it is like a dried-out river in time of drought

Sometimes it is like the ocean rich and strong

Life is a journey no matter where it takes you

You will have to survive

It could be in a jungle ~ It could be in a pit

When Jesus is with you, it feels like a paradise within

Life is a journey and the passage is free

Just keep holding on to Jesus and He will see you through

Life is a journey so stay on the right route

THE TROUBLED SOUL

Drifting off to distant places within her mind

She has travelled many places within her mind

Within her mind, she seems to have taken a thousand steps to see places that she would normally see when she took a ship.

Her normal would return once in-awhile, but she does not seem to be at home here most of the time, within her mind

I have often thought if I could only see where she is within her mind.

I would understand why she drifted off to places in her mind

NO MERCY BY THY SELF

Have you ever sat back and placed yourself in the courtroom of your life to view your cases of charges and acts committed that no one else is aware of but you and God?

Have you ever tried to try your own case and found out that you are as guilty as sinners are and the penalty of that sin is your own conscience and the burden to carry to death?

Have you ever tried giving your sentence to others to lessen your burden and conscience but found out that they increase your sentence with pain and sorrow?

Have you come to realize in the courtroom of your life that there is no mercy in self but only condemnation?

Have you come to realize that your sentence of burden, guilt, and conscience along with pain and sorrow are just there to drive you insane, but by God's grace and mercy, you remain sane to declare Him a winner in your life?

Have you also come to the realization that the man from Galilee took your place of being convicted for all that you have done; by His declaring that it is finished by His Father up above; that we can be one in the spirit?

Have you come to realize that in the courtroom of your life where the Lord is Judge that there is no condemnation? No condemnation at all for those who love the Lord.

THE STRENGTH OF FRIENDSHIP

My sister, my friend

I have promised myself to love you until my mind refuses to function and my heart becomes like a rock and my eyes no longer behold you.

My friendship is without a price; The love I am extending is from my heart through Jesus the Christ.

I can't be biased with my talk; it will only flatter your ego and weaken my heart.

I may not see you as much but this friendship is that of a bond that will not be broken.

I will love you from a distance with a prayer -- a prayer that God will hear and keep my friend, because He, too, cares as much.

BESETTING PRIDE

I met a man who was not very strong

His sickness has kept him down,

His faith was not that strong. An educator he was with his many degrees, yet he felt prey to adversity.

One thing led to another in his life; let him look to his own strength! Within that strength, he appeared strong; that strength became his reward. Forgotten are the things he has been taught, such as work and faith walk hand in hand. One without the other is pitiable of a weakened soul.

I met a man who was not very strong

His sickness has kept him down,

His faith was not very strong.

Being a weakened man and too far gone in his ways, he declined to believe that grace can be obtained by surrendering the self-indulging man he became; pride kept him bound with his hardened heart of stone. Misery became his reward for negating the One greater than he; there was no peace he could obtain; home he went to an early grave.

THE FIRST HELLO, TO FOREVER

Yesterday, you were strangers, until you unfolded the mystery of love lurking in the air with your first hello

Today, together your hearts are sharing a space in this universe as you pray that what you have found will never end

Tomorrow, you will be awake by the grace of God, in unity with the love that is given to you

Forever is until eternity. With many Winters, Springs, Summers, and Falls, including droughts, floods, and storms, your love will go on by trusting God in the midst, of it all

THE CARIBBEAN SUN

Laying on the beach in the pelting Caribbean Island sun, viewing the ocean flow of the raging sea, seeing the waves whaled as if to touch the clouds has captivated my emotions. As I lay there in the basking sun, I thought of how refreshing the flow of salty water would make me feel; if only I dared myself to brave the whaling tides to feel the coolness of the ocean water on my warm body from the pelting sun.

The title mother is very special -- being a
mother and having a mother, it's a gift and
Also, a reward that crowns a
mom's heart with love

IT'S MOM AND HER HEART OF GOLD

The love that flows from a mother's heart is like the heaven and the stars; it's also as the moon that brightens the path of her children. The flowering garden of her soul is watered by every tear she shed as she uttered prayer of guidance and prosperity as her children's inheritance. Thriving, the hope for every step she takes is for the blessings she hoped for will continue to behold her offspring. No fight too tough, no battle too vigorous a task for her to challenge that victory be declared.

The love of a mother is that of a rose garden in full bloom. Bright, beautiful, yet delicate. No! A mother never wishes to think of the negative but a mother's heart can be torn by the possibilities; you know what I mean -- sorrow and grief do lurk in the air. But the love of a mother never fails even after the impossible.

The love that flows from a mother's heart to yours deserves a special treat of empathy, compassion, and recognition for the cushion she is in the time of comfort; the sponge she is to absorb all that her children have and had put her through; and her love never tarnishes. It's mom and her heart of gold.

Dear Mother, we are blessed having you as our mom.

As we journey through the growth of motherhood with children of our own, we have come to realize and acknowledge your joy, your pain, your struggles, your accomplishments, your hard work, and achievements. You have done it -- walking, running, and crying yourself through the process. Now you are looking at us these many years later,

walking the distance with our children as you have done with us and saying it was worth it all.

Mother, our dear Mother, we have seen and felt the love in all you have done. And we thank you.

Such love and nurture as you have given us has flown into the lives of our children. For all the years you held and comforted us and filling the gaps, we thank you.

Now that we have reaped the legacies of a mother who is queen of her children's heart, we pray that one day we will be able to receive the reward of dear Mother from our children's hearts.

WE APPRECIATE YOU, MOM

Greetings, Mother; love, hugs and kisses to you

From your children all appreciations are due

We have seen your sacrifices

We have witnessed your tears

Yes! The frowns upon your face are also evidence of your thoughts and burdens you bare.

The wants and needs of your children became your sole priority because of your motherly love and ways.

Mother dear, oh! Mother dear, you have sacrificed for us in millions of ways

Now that we are able, to recognize how low you would go that your children may go high, we are singing your praise with a heartfelt thank you.

Thank you for holding on for us even when you could have given up

Thank you for believing in us when we felt discouraged

Thank you for being our strength when we grew weak

Thank you for continuing to praying for us when we ceased to do so for ourselves

Most of all, we thank you for being mom!

HER CHILDREN CALLED
HER BLESSED

She is a woman of virtue and dignity

She stands tall in her grace with such pride

She will follow through whatever her promises would be

She lifts her head up with all dignity and pride, declaring us as her prize

She is the woman who births us to life

She is the woman who cries and prays over us

She makes a fuss for us to walk right

She scolds and molds us and she even influences us with her ways

She teaches us more than she would know each and everyday

Because of her, we have grown into the adult that we can appreciate

We owe it all to you, Mother

MOTHERHOOD

Motherhood is a lifetime achievement

It comes with no degree

But requires qualification of

Love, Patience and Sacrifice

Mothers, you have displayed such qualities to your children

Therefore, a special day is dedicated to you

MOTHERS

Mothers are pillows in times of comfort
Mothers are hankies in times of sorrow
Mothers are a special gift for every child
Mothers are you and me
Mothers are mothers
For that's who we are created to be

Dear Mother, when I think of the things
that you do even when you are feeling blue,
I dream of Mother's Day and of honoring you
with a crown, to erase the frown and a banner
that says, "Mom, you are the best"

I BEHOLD YOU, MOTHER

Words are not enough to say

How much I am blessed when it comes to acknowledging that I still have you, Mother, on the surface of this earth

Knowing that each day that comes to an end, you are, able to lie down to take a rest. And to each morning that rises and you arose with the knowledge of your place of motherhood in this world of temptation and greed

We, your children, called you blessed mother in spite, of being cursed with pain at child birth. Not to mention the trial and test that comes with the growth of us, your children. But in the end, a crown of love and pride with a blessed assurance that you have done your best is placed upon your heart.

PRAY ON, MOTHERS

The picture of a praying mother is hard to erase, not when you are constantly seeing her giving praise, her praise for love, joy, and prosperity. The things she longed for her child to have and behold and be. As the years go by, those things may not be as she prayed them to be. It has not yet come into being. Don't be in despair, woman who bears the child. God's promises haven't ended because your hope and expectation are not what you set your child's destiny to be.

The picture of a praying mother is hard to erase, not when you are constantly seeing her giving praise; pray on, Mother, and give God the honor and the praise. He will set the format for your child by His grace. Don't despair, oh, praying mother!

God's arms are always in place.

DEDICATED TO FATHERS

"Fathers represent strength; a
provider and a mentor"

THE STRENGTH OF A FATHER

We have watched you, Dad, throughout the years

The way you stand tall in your strength, not letting fear or hardship detour you from your goals -- us, your children.

The time you spent ushering words of wisdom to heal our wounded heart

The encouragement you gave to us, to help guide us through life

The provisions you have provided day in and day out

We would like you to know that they have not gone unnoticed and we thank you.

Your love has sparked our lives in so many ways. On this day of recognition, we are saying to you, Dad, thank you for being the star you are. But most of all, to our Father above for giving us you, our dad

A FATHER'S PRAYER

My Father in heaven, I did not know you then as I know you now; through life's journey, you have brought me through.

I want to thank you, Father, for when I did not know you, however you have pulled me through. Things are not the same today as they were yesterday, for me. Today, I have learned to praise you and I have learned the meaning of agape.

Your love for me, your intimate ways of knowing me, and, my surrendering to your unfailing love -- My Father in heaven, I want to thank you for being my Father so that I can be that father to my children.

"OUR HEAVENLY FATHER"

I have a Father as no other father I know

He is with me all the time and go wherever I go. My Father is not of this world, but he has catered to my every need

As an earthly father living here on land

I will give a hand to those who see me

and know me as a man of God. I will take their hand and lead them to the Heavenly One -- the Father of all fathers who wants all men to be strong.

O you who hear prayer, to you
all men will come. Psalm 65:2

WE ARE THE PRODUCT

We are the product of our fore-parents who abide in the valleys and climbed the hills, toiling from sun up until sun down, suffering physical and mental abuse That we will be free.

We are the product of our fore-parents who may have questioned their faults, their self-worth. However, they suffered in their inability to be free, toiling from sun up to sun down, not for themselves, but for us, the children, the future generation.
That we will be free.

We are the product of our fore-parents who did not tasted the sweetness of freedom they have toiled for from sun up until sun down.
That we will be free, free to inherit the legacy of their sweat, tears and pain We, we are the product.

STRIVING TO DO RIGHT

I am a black man
Don't you see I'm trying to do things right?
There is a struggle
Years of struggle should be getting me down but I've surely put up a fight

You see, I want to be right
I have practiced day and night
So that I'll be good in your sight
It does not matter if I'm not quite right
Because to you I'm not that bright

Although you have tried to put me down so many times
I always raised up with a light
Yes! I am black
But don't you see my dignity means a lot to me?

WE HEARD THE DRUMS!

My brothers and sisters, don't you hear the freedom bells ringing?

They toll so strong that it could break the shackled heart. The ringing is of freedom; dong, they go.

Gong, gong, they go on, "I am ringing for you; it's a time of jubilee," says the tolling bells

Wait! But, but, are we free?

We, the people, who were once enslaved are free? Wow! That's what they believe; freed by what measure?

Blind eyes do not see the chains, the chains of rejection and depression by the indifferences. By the belief of being free, we should be dancing to the sound of the bells: dong, dong.

No, no, we will not dance; we are still fighting the fight of equality and acceptance.

No, no! It's not freedom; it's a touch of sympathy with no obligation to any further foresight of recognition.

I dream of a time of redemption, not only from the souls that lack compassion, but also from those who dance the dance of privilege to the tune of distance and scorn in their hearts.

However, in the frontline, they declared acceptance because they know the value of our worth.

I hear the tolling of the bells, sounding out ding-dongs of promises of peace, joy, and prosperity.

Yes! I hear the freedom bells ringing, but my heart is feeling the weight of disappointment.

The bells are tolling; our feet have been routed by the sound of drums declaring: March on! March on against injustice,

March on against poverty,

March on against discrimination and

brutality; march on, march on!

Our feet are marching on to the sound and beating of the drums; boom, boom, boom, here we come.

We are marching on; boom, boom, boom

The sound of wanting to be free; boom, boom, boom.

The sounding of the drums!

What man can live and not see death or save
himself from the power of the grave?
Psalm 89:48

CRY NOT FOR ME

Cry not for me, my beautiful one
Not because my days are done
Your days should not be filled with sorrow because I have no tomorrow

My life -- I have lived to the fullest here on earth, but now that I am put under ground, please continue to trod upon this land

God has given you the continuation of your life because you are yet to be called
Yes, my dearest one, cry not for me because I am gone

GOD IS THERE

As memories overflow your mind of the day your loved one went home and everything seems to stop functioning in your world, God is there

As that memorable day becomes faded and each day becomes brighter in your heart, God is there

Memories of moments shared become embraceable, loveable gestures more understandable. The treasures you shared are more cherished. The foundations that were set are more acceptable; God is there

Your pillow of sorrows weeping in the night will become joy of abundant blessings in the morn; God is there

Your inheritance from our loving King is great in abundant love

He is always there; be comforted in His arms

Don't take it to heart now that I depart, without a kiss or farewell to those that were near or far. My name has been called as I know it would, but my goodbye or farewell was not able to be said. I knew that you prayed for my healing, but I was not praying for deliverance from death but for God's welcoming arms to embrace me home. My love ones, while I rest, you continue your life journey. You have only, to believe that prayer and love will see you through. I leave you Jesus; He cared for me then; He will do the same for you, too; just don't procrastinate in embracing Him.

FAREWELL TO A DAD

There are times in our lives we bid farewell to our loved ones for one reason or another. The saddest farewell of all is the final one, bringing back memories of time shared. The voice, the tone, and the sounds that we came to know. The laughers, the jokes shared. That smile or possibly a hug that said you are special. The receptivity of good times and the unmentionable fears. For all the qualities he had, he was just a man you called dad.

In his imperfect ways, he loved

In his unpredictable ways, he loved

Hold tight to the memories that fit you well. Let go of what would have and should have; embrace the memories of the man known as your dad.

His farewell was final; Your journey will continue, live on. Love, laugh and pray; your today, too, will become a memory someday.

A MISSED LOVED ONE

Life is just a passing time on this earth; how we live that life is up to you and me. With outstretched arms, we can embrace a lonely soul; with tender words we can warm someone's heart. With a listening ear, we can help erase someone's pain.

My loved one, now that you have gone, I realized that your embrace I have not felt or your face I have not seen for so many years. My holding the position of adulthood in this world has not lessened the anxiety of my will to be independent but made it more demanding.

My loved one, not that I had not tried to see your face before you go;

however, procrastination has worked overtime. Now that you are gone to a better place, knowing that you had found comfort in God's grace here on earth is a comfort to my heart.

BONUS ~ STORIES

THE THOUGHTS OF A TREE

Then all the trees of the forest will
sing for joy; Psalm 96:12

As the season changes from those cold blistering days of winter to the somewhat conflicting mood of early spring; where the transition seems to birth a debate between the two climates; in regards of the two, who will be the winner of the allotted time that needs to please or displease the hearts of the human's race? For the lovers of the cold who refuse to accept that old man, winter is bidding them farewell for the time being; whereas the anticipated spring lovers are embracing and welcoming the transformation from the gloomy days to those of promises of new birth and warm sunlight.

But for us trees, it doesn't matter; nature will take its course. For instance, some of us trees are standing unclothed because the weaving of materials hasn't come together for the designer's work to refresh the eyes of those who will be flattered by the producer's handiwork.

Now that the somewhat warmth of the sun can be felt in the early stages of development in spring, the sunlight glows upon my bareness and it feels good as I reflect on the past days of old man winter's chills and snow. On snowy days, our covering was all white. It felt wonderful to be covered in coating of white to please the eyes of those that took time to admire us, however, that, too, was gone in no time -- melted away -- and we were uncovered once again. I also realized that among us, some neighbors have maintained their clothing of green throughout the time of old man winter, and it had me curious if they were richer, or if they were more favored by the designer. I wondered if that's the reason why they are woven in qualities that stay ever so green? During the blistering cold time, the feelings became downcast from not having the frequent visit of my feathery friends; I became saddening from the thoughts that I will not see them as before; as you will notice, my branches are lacking the covering and I appear unattractive without my leaves.

It was refreshing yesterday when I felt the strong ray of the sun giving me hope that spring is claiming its potion as the season that will stand strong. I cannot wait for the flow of heaven's crystal stream flowing down on me; with it will be a feeling of warmth with its soothing flow that will nurture my trunk for the new beginning of what has been at rest within my branches. I often glance at my fellow trees and wonder if they, too, have survived the harshness of the winter the way I did and now they are trying to strive within the coolness of the early spring. I know I am not looking like much now, however, I am anticipating the future -- when I will be decked out in my flushing green leaves. My friends, the birds, will very soon be kissing me and building their homes among my splendid green leaves and I will be able to witness the birth of their new ones. The squirrels will also visit sometime. There are times some unpleasant bow-wows do displeasing things to my trunk; I just accept it and hope for the rain to come. There is something else I anticipate and that's my human friends stopping by and taking pictures right alongside me.

Oh! I am looking forward to the enforcement of spring and the blooming of everything around me -- so beautiful, yes! With the flowers it will be; after so many weeks and days of rest, oh! I am going to be glowing with my best. Goodbye, winter; hello spring. I am so happy you are here again. I am hoping when summer makes its presence, I will enjoy flourishing in the sun and hope for some crystal flow from above to refresh me from the scorching sun. Well! I am just a tree, hoping to have some spring into summer fun.

To Be Deceived
or
Not to Be Deceived

"Do not be deceived: God is not mocked, for
whatever one sows, that he also reaps." Gal. 6:7

Really! Really is all that seems to come
to mind when the sound of the word
regularly echoes back at me.
                                    -Paulette Livingston.

Really, did Gregg analyze my face in-depth to
conclude that it is regular and that I am plain? I
definitely! know that I am no Cleopatra or Monalisa
and I certainly did not declare that I wanted to look
like either of the two when he came at me the first
time we met. I remember our first encounter as if it
was only yesterday.

As I stood waiting for a cab, he came unto me with
all smiles and glows in those big brown eyes of his.
His charms were irresistible and macho, his approach
was inviting and embracing. He would not accept
no for an answer when he had asked for my name

and phone number. Therefore, I relented and gave it to him. I was impressed with him and I was more flattered when I received a call within the hour after departing from him. The conversation was that of compliments and flattery that came from him and it boosted my ego. He told me that he loved what he saw and he would love to get to know me better. I agreed to the request and we took it from there. Thereafter, we went on several dates that left me with feelings of being special, as if I was his queen. Before we began to live together, we spent many hours talking and texting each other nights and days; he was always there for me which led us to decide that it would be good if Gregg moved in with me. The decision to me then seemed perfect, especially when it came to the special bond I believed we shared and our talks of the future together.

The thought of us ever being apart did not seem possible. I believed we were perfect together and so I adapted to the idea that sometime soon in the future, I would be Mrs. Gregg Washington.

Wow! Can you imagine at this time how I felt after overhearing Gregg with someone on the phone discussing me? My thoughts were of how foolish I have been to be blinded by his charms. How could someone of his features be attracted to someone such as I. I consulted myself. A plain-Jane -- that's what I have been called most of my younger life. I couldn't wrong him to declare my face regular and to add insult to injury, it was not his intention to make me his wife. He said to the person on the other side of the phone-line. The extent of his conversation was not comforting to my ears either; it was an acknowledgement that he was only spending time with me until his future wife finished her studies. I couldn't bear to hear any more, therefore, I went back out for a walk.

After leaving work a couple hours earlier that day, I could not wait to get home to be in the arms of whom I thought was my life partner. What I overheard kept repeating in my head as I walked along the street absent-mindedly. I have been used all along; he had been using me. Here I was, believing I was all he needed, not knowing that he was only passing time with me, because apparently, he felt sorry for me.

This plain-Jane, this face! It's the same face that my father and siblings had tried to change over the years. My father had often reminded me as, long as I can remember that I am the least of his children, with an appearance such as mine. "Where is the ugly one?" he would inquire of my half-brother and sisters. I was the black sheep of the family. I was a product of a fly-by-night relationship between my mother and father. According to my father, my mother was a very good dancer. With her being a good dancer, he had chosen her to be his partner at the club that they had met each other one Saturday night for the first time. During the process of the night, my mom had gotten drunk and he took her home to her parent's house; in that event he ended up sleeping over; her parents were not home at the time; they were away on vacation. This was the explanation my father had given to his wife of my existence. The detail of his story continued. My father explained that two months later, after that Saturday night experience, they ran into each other at a store; that was when my mother took the opportunity to inform him of her pregnancy. My father said my mother claimed that he was responsible for her being pregnant, therefore, he accepted it. He said at that time he was not married and had no other kids. Therefore, he was proud of the idea of being a father until his family and friends began to instill doubts in his mind. They told him my mother loved to party, that she would get drunk in the process. They questioned if he was certain that the baby was his.

As Paulette continued to reflect on her past, she recalled the woman she knew as her mother.

"Mother was the only person who had loved me. That was what I believed until I met Gregg. But now, once again, I will hold on to what I believed then. My mother was the only person who loved me. I don't recall much of my mother whose name was Patsy; however, what I recalled of her life with me told of a mother who adored her child and lived a life that reflected that love. My mother was a fashionable woman who loved to dress. That I recalled and it stayed with me, and as she loved to dress herself up, she did the same for me. I remember she took me to almost everywhere she went. On the days that she worked, Mother would take me to stay with a lady she called Miss Catty. Miss Catty was living not too far away from the school where Mother taught. At about eight o'clock each school day, I would be picked up from Miss Catty's home by the school bus and returned after school to be picked up by my mother. Mother was a pretty and petite woman who had walked strong in her strength.

As a child, I believed that my mother could do everything. She was a junior high school teacher and she was a lover of books. Patsy, my mother, would read to me every night and in return she would let me read to her. She was also playful and we had fun playing together. I knew that my mother loved me; everything she did said it and she used to tell me so every day. Mother would often held me close to her and squeeze me lovingly and patted my cheeks.

I was nine years old when my mother died. She was killed in a car accident on her way from work to get me from Miss Catty's home. That was the day love left my life. My mother's family did not want me and I guess it was for the same reason that my father made obvious every day I had lived with him and his family until I left his sight at the early age of seventeen.

The friends I had over the years at school tried their best to make life rewarding for me by lifting my spirit up with positive encouragements. The ones that were not friends, the bullies, added insults that were equal to that of my father's. As I matured, my spirit improved with the glow of life around me. When it came to choosing a profession, my first choice was teaching -- a gesture in honoring my mother's chosen profession, however, I found nursing as my calling.

At the age of twenty-five, I became a registered nurse. Within time, this plain-Jane appearance improved with the use of make-up. I believed I was doing good in the appearance department; at least, that's what my eyes told me and the compliments that I received confirmed it. Now, after those many years of being undermined and insulted for the lack of being attractive according to men's standard, now, coming to the realization that the man who said he loved me has become a reflection of my father and what I had endured for being the child that he didn't love. The man that I had spent two-plus years with has decided that I was not the woman he would have for a wife by declaring I was too plain and my face was regular. The nerve of him. I know that I am fearfully and wonderfully designed by God according to the bible. Therefore, I will not allow him to let me feel insecure at this time of my life, as I was before; I am living and I will go on surviving with the help of God.

The information Paulette had obtained from Greg's conversation on the phone had her thinking of the position she was in regarding Greggs plan for her in the future. Therefore, she opened her mind to her new predicament. Throughout the duration of time, Paulette kept what she had overheard to herself. She had not confronted Gregg about what she had learned but had decided to play his game along with him.

Paulette began to work on her game plan for her future. The first thing she did a week after hearing Gregg's conversation was, she opened a post office box only for her mails. She closed her bank account that he had access to and opened another account with a different bank. She cancelled her credit cards account that he had card to. Paulette did not know when the relationship would come to an end officially. However, in her mind, it already had.

For a few years, she had played with the idea of becoming a nurse practitioner, but after she met Gregg, she delayed it because it would mean spending less time with him. Now, she would be stepping out to claim her right to move on, to achieve what she was destined to become.

Six months after her knowledge of being used by her boyfriend, Paulette, viewed a three-bedroom house on Long Island that was for sale on the market. It was a long way from her apartment in Brooklyn, however, she applied for the house; four months later, she became a home-owner. Within a month, she was in the house. For a starter, Paulette furnished the living-room and closed off the rest of the house except for the kitchen and bathroom. She then took partial residency there. A few days out of the week, she would stay at her new home for a couple of hours after work before heading to her apartment in Brooklyn. On Wednesdays, she was able to sleep over at her house without attracting any suspicion to herself. It so happened that on Wednesdays, Gregg claimed that his brother worked the night shift on his job, therefore, Gregg had to stay with their mother who had been diagnosed with Alzheimer's.

Paulette had never met Gregg's mother throughout the time of their relationship. On few occasions, Paulette took the initiative of offering her assistant to help Gregg to attend to his mother but was turned down whenever she extended her offer. Paulette had applied to a few nursing colleges to become a nurse practitioner with the understanding that it would put a strain on the relationship that Gregg believed was going on between them; but in truth, Paulette was playing his game. Her feelings for Gregg have now been demolished; she was now being curious as to what extent he was willing to go with the lies of his love for her. Her curiosity was not far in being shed a light upon.

It was one evening as they sat watching the news; Paulette told Gregg that she was going back to college to further her studies to become a nurse practitioner. He clicked the television off before he turned and faced her with the question, "What for? You are already a professional nurse."

He further told her that if she went back to college, it would mean she would not have time for him and that she should reconsider doing so. Furthermore, he told her that he would not be able to assist her financially at all. Paulette told him she already planned on taking out a loan if necessary. Gregg then clicked the television on, and turned the volume up, and tuned her out.

Sometime in the middle of the following year, after Paulette began her studies, Gregg approached Paulette and told her that he could not continue with the relationship. He blamed her for his decision by stating that he wanted a woman who would be there for him. Paulette told him she respected his decision but she was thinking about her future and that he had not given her a reason to do otherwise; therefore, she had made the decision to pave her own way. She also told him she would leave the apartment by the end of that month. But Gregg insisted that he should be the one to go. Paulette didn't argue the point, however, the following day, she gave the landlord two weeks, notice.

Two days later, when Gregg was at work, Paulette took her personal belongings which included a few of her clothes and left everything else behind.

She changed her phone number. The previous year, Paulette had changed from the hospital that Gregg knew she was working. To the best of Paulette's knowledge, she had covered all her tracks from having a surprise visit from Gregg.

Six years later, as destiny would have it, Paulette and Gregg crossed paths. By this time, Paulette was a nurse practitioner working with one of Long Island's recognized hospitals and, also doing part-time at a neighborhood clinic as an assistant nurse in Queens, along with her fiancé who so happened to be the head doctor at that clinic.

One evening, Gregg walked into the clinic with a child, about four years old, in his arms with a woman walking along beside him. As they entered, they were waited upon by the receptionist who took their information before they sat and waited to be called. When it was their turn for the doctor to see the child, the nurse who happened to be Paulette, came out to escort the family to the waiting-room.

"Mr.& Mrs. Washington, the doctor will see your daughter now; come this way please."

When Gregg saw it was Paulette, his eyes expanded at the view. He could not believe he was looking at the woman whom he thought was not qualified in the appearance bracket to be his wife even though he had not told her so personally. Paulette, on the other hand, continued to perform her duties in a professional manner and didn't show any indication she recognized him. However, Paulette did sneakily take glances at his wife, and thought to herself, "She is as plain as I was. I guess, as the saying goes, 'beauty is in the eyes of the beholder.' Well, she has him."

When the doctor was through diagnosing the child, the parents were told she would be okay with a few days rest and with Tylenol to reduce her temperature; they were further informed that it was nothing much to worry about, but if she did not feel better within those few days, they should bring her back. The parents thanked the doctor. Gregg nodded at Paulette before exiting the examining room. Paulette had noticed that throughout the time the family was in the room, Gregg was eyeing her and she remained firm in ignoring him.

A week later, Paulette saw Gregg again; this time, he was alone. Paulette was by herself that day which was a change to her and her fiancé's routine of commuting together with his car. On that day, he was asked to cover for another resident doctor at the hospital. Therefore, Paulette was able to have that encounter with Gregg without the presence of her soon-to-be husband; she was on her own. As Paulette was walking toward her car, she heard Gregg's voice call her name. When she turned and faced him, he was standing by the parking lot for the clinic.

With folded arms, he stood looking at Paulette before he spoke to her. He began speaking by complimenting her on her appearance, "You are looking good in all the right places," were his words to her before he extended his regret for not being supportive of her and her dreams.

He further implied that she appeared to be doing well for herself before he inquired of her, of how she was able to walk away and leave the apartment with everything behind. Paulette then related to him the phone conversation she heard the day she had gotten home early from work -- when he told someone on the other end of the line that she, Paulette, was not qualified in the looks category to be his wife. Gregg stood looking at her with disbelief. When he spoke, it was that of a man having a soul-searching experience.

"You heard all of that and you didn't accost me about it, you continued living with me even then?"

Paulette responded to him, "Yes! I did, didn't I; however, I did not just remain in place and mourned my sorrows; I remained to get motivated and built myself up. You were certain that you had the upper hand on me, that you didn't notice the changes taking place around you. My returning to college was me setting the pace between you and me. Your phone conversation opened my eyes to your plot of buying time with me until your chosen wife-to-be finished with her studies. Therefore, armed with such knowledge, I concluded that if I continue with my studies, I will benefit from accomplishing my dream of being a nurse practitioner and you will be deprived of your bed warmer. And just as I predicted, goodbye would not fall short of being presented; but what you did not realize is that I had left you long before you said it. Oh! and I will also outline the fact that it didn't take another man to do so. I may be plain but not stupid. I did it all by myself, along with the grace of God. All that I am and have become -- it's all thanks to the glory of God."

Gregg stood with his hand folded staring at Paulette. She continued to speak once again. "So! Gregg, I am not mad at you, I thank you, but I thank the Lord for allowing me to overheard your phone conversation when I did. Who knows; I would now be losing years being regretful and pining over a broken heart. Now, I am in a different place, in a couple of weeks, I will be marrying a Godly and professional man who didn't measure me by my looks but by my qualities. Goodbye, Gregg, go home and take care of your family, I wish you all the best."

Paulette walked the few steps to her car with her head held high and a smile of accomplishment on her face as she opened the door to her late model BMW, an engagement gift from her husband-to-be. As she stepped in and closed the door, switched the engine on, Paulette lifted her head and whispered a prayer of thanksgiving before driving off to the house she has made a home. Not once did she looked back at her past standing where she had left him.

ABOUT THE AUTHOR

The author stood looking at her reflection in the mirror hanged on the entrance door to her room. As she looked at herself in the mirror, she spoke to her reflection. "Mirror, mirror, looking at you and seeing me has awakened the light in my eyes which shines from the glow within my being, and I love what I'm seeing."

To which the reflection in the mirror replied, "You have walked within your strength. You have stood tall at your height; years have done you well into today and tomorrow is yet to tell."

The author's reflection has spoken her truth. Juliet a petite woman who gained strength and has structured herself from the past with the determination of moving on in life by embracing nature and the wonders of God. There she hopes to continue to be comforting and encouraging others.

As a mother, her prayers and dreams are to continue sowing good seeds in the lives of her daughters and now her grandchildren, as well as other young people she encounters, and, also adults.

As for having a relationship with her Lord and Savior, it allows Juliet to exercise the grace she has encountered with the Savior to others.

The writing of this book is Juliet's way of sharing the gift she has received and poetically communicating her feelings along with her trust and belief that the Savior is and always will be in the mix of everything, He is, in our lives at all times, Yes! His ever presence is there for you to accept and embrace Him.

*"and to know this love that surpasses
knowledge that you may be filled to the
measure of all the fullness of God"*
(Eph.3:19)